Are You Listening, Lord?

Reflections for Christian Teen Girls

Mary Ann Kerl

LANGMARC PUBLISHING

Are You Listening, Lord?
Reflections for Teen-age Christian Girls

By Mary Ann Kerl

Editor: Renée Hermanson
Cover Graphics: Michael L. Qualben
Cover Photography: Stern T. Hatcher
Photographer: Stern T. Hatcher

Scripture quotations are from the Holy Bible,
New International Version.
Copyright © 1973, 1978, 1984 International Bible Society.
Used by permission of Zondervan Bible Publishers.

LangMarc Publishing

P.O. 33817, San Antonio, TX 78265

Printed in the United States of America

Library of Congress Cataloguing in Publication Data in Process
ISBN: 1-880292-14-9

Dedication

To my Mother,
Lula Wheeler,
and a special friend,
Loretta Browning,
for their Christian love and support

Thank you

to photographer, Stern T. Hatcher

Thank you to Katie Wheeless,

Jeneen Boyd, Mrs. Boyd

and Spencer Kerr

for allowing us to photograph them

Contents

WHO ARE YOU?..8
  The Greatest Gift 9
  Who Are You? 11
  Hero 13
FEELINGS...15
  Feelings Aren't Sins 16
  Hurts 18
  Contentment 20
FRIENDSHIP..22
  Selecting Friends 23
  Promises, Promises 25
  Me Forgive Me? 27
LOOK ON THE BRIGHT SIDE 29
  Bright Side 30
  Is Your Life One Total Maze? 32
  Change 34
LET'S HAVE FUN 36
  Can Christians Have Fun? 37
  Drugs Aren't Funny...Or Fun! 39
DAY BY DAY 41
  Daydreaming 42
  Now...44
  Excited About Your Future Career? 46
  Treating Yourself...48
BEAUTY INSIDE OR OUTSIDE.......................... 50
  Getting Beautiful 51
  Self-Esteem 53
  Special Gifts 55
DATING 57
  How Can I Get a Date? 58
  Love...Is It Money? 60
  Guys and Sex 62
  Saying No Can Be Beautiful 64
  Abortion 66
  Homosexuality 68

PARENTS 70
    Parents! Who Needs Them? 71
    Demands 73
    Patience...Nice Word...75
    Stress, Stress, and More Stress! 77
LONELINESS 79
    Loneliness 80
    What About Cults? 82
    Strength 84
GOD IN YOUR LIFE 86
    Keeping God in Your Life 87
    Loving God 89
    Faith 91
    Prayer 93
ARE YOU LISTENING, LORD? 95

About the Author..96

If unavailable at your local bookstore,
find out on page 96 how to order
Are Your Listening, Lord?

Preface

Meet the girls in this book who have faced some pretty heavy stuff in their lives. Listen to what they say. Some of their thoughts may surprise you. You can learn from them. Their names have been changed to protect their privacy, but they're real girls just like you—girls who have a lot of tough issues to face in today's society. You may have been through some difficult problems already in your life. Or perhaps you are in the middle of a crisis as you read this.

It is my prayer that these reflections will help you establish a firm and loving relationship with Jesus Christ. I hope you will be comfortable enough to tell Him your problems. That kind of relationship is vital to successful Christian living!

True, Jesus walked this earth as a human long ago, nearly two thousand years ago, but don't let that fool you. Through the beautiful and mysterious Holy Spirit, God can reveal Jesus Christ to you in a way that is personal and just right for today.

So try our challenges and suggestions—and talk to Jesus as you never have before. He's waiting, ready to listen to you.

Remember that the next time you ask, "Are You Listening, Lord?" His answer to that question is always the same: YES!

Mary Ann Kerl

Who Are You?

The Greatest Gift

God gave you a gift more precious and greater than any gift you will ever receive from anyone else.

What is that gift? You!

Think about it. What is greater to you than you? Your life is precious. You are an unrepeatable miracle. No one ever has been or ever will be you. You are unique, made in God's image. There is no way anybody will ever replace you. You cannot be cloned.

Isn't that great?

Doesn't it make you feel special?

God wants everyone to appreciate His creation. In other words, God wants you to enjoy yourself.

How?

Not by using drugs.

Or having premarital sex.

But by living an active and productive Christian life, to live your life abundantly.

In John 10:10-11 it says Jesus came into this world so you can have an abundant life. The verse reads: "...I have come that they may have life, and have it to the full. I am the good shepherd. The good shepherd lays down his life for the sheep."

"Wait a minute," you may say, "if that's the case then what's wrong with having pot once in a while or having sex with someone you *really* like?" After all, everybody's doing it!

Okay. Stop and think about it. Get serious. Don't you have to admit using drugs and having premarital sex leads to abuse? To abuse is defined in Webster as to hurt, mistreat, insult, deceive.

Remember how the prodigal son in one of Jesus' stories abused his gift of life and how he sought forgiveness. Let this parable be a lesson to value so you will use your gift of life wisely. Sometime read the parable in Luke 15:11-32 for review.

✝SCRIPTURE:

"...I have come that they may have life, have it to the full." John 10:10b

⅋

REFLECTION:

1) Think of someone you know who uses their life wisely. What is it about that person that you admire?

2) Are you using your life wisely at the present time? If not, what do you need to do to change?

⅋

✔ CHALLENGE:

Appreciate yourself by doing one or more of the following:

• Write God a thank-you letter today in your diary. Thank Him for the greatest gift you've ever received—yourself!

• Go to the mirror and take a good look at yourself. Tell yourself you're number one, that you count because God made you and He doesn't make junk.

• Then ask Him to help you live your life wisely.

Who Are You?

Go to the mirror. See who you are on the outside. Blonde hair, blue eyes. Or maybe you have dark hair and dark brown eyes and dark skin. Or red hair with some freckles splashed across your nose and cheeks.

But who are you inside?

What is it that turns you on? What makes you tick? What excites you? Bores you? Makes you angry?

You can't answer these questions by looking in the mirror. It takes sincere introspection, searching inside yourself to find the answers.

Study who you are inside. You may find a number of things you like about yourself. You may see some things you don't like so well, things you want to work on.

Do you suppose Jesus asked Himself the same questions?

In John 13:5 it says: "After that, he poured water into a basin and began to wash his disciples' feet, drying them with the towel that was wrapped around him." By washing His disciples' feet, Jesus was saying He was a servant. The Bible stresses that Jesus—who is Almighty God, Ruler of the Universe—came into this world not to be waited on by people, but to serve humankind.

"But how can I be a servant?" you may ask. "After all, Jesus lived a long time ago. A lot of things have changed since then."

That's true, but we can still serve Jesus today. Take a look at our challenges on the next page.

† SCRIPTURE:

"I tell you the truth, no servant is greater than his master, nor is a messenger greater than the one who sent him. Now that you know these things, you will be blessed if you do them. I am not referring to all of you; I know those I have chosen." John 13:16-18a

REFLECTION:
1) Analyze your Christian life now. Look *inside* yourself. How are you serving Jesus now?

2) Is "serving" an area of your life that needs work? If it is, what do you need to do?

✔CHALLENGE:

Serve Jesus by doing one or more of the following:

• Take a basket of fresh wild flowers to an elderly person in a nursing home. If you don't know anyone, ask your minister for a name. Or offer the flowers as a table decoration.

• Invite that unpopular girl to your home one day after school.

• Volunteer to do something for your next youth group meeting such as cleaning up after refreshments.

• Do something nice for someone today—like helping a younger brother or sister make a craft.

Hero

Who is your hero? Maybe one person comes to mind. Or maybe there are several people you are especially fond of. But have you ever thought of yourself as a hero too?

No, I'm not kidding. Stop and think about it. God already thinks of you as a hero. You are His masterpiece! You are a miracle of God's handiwork, fashioned after the very image of God Himself. Think of yourself accordingly. Don't put yourself down.

You are special. When I was a teen, I often complained about myself.

"My hair doesn't look right," I used to say. Or I would complain, "I wish I were taller!" Or still another complaint of mine was, "Why, why do I have to have freckles?"

Later, as I grew up, I began to realize that when I made those statements, I was actually putting God down. I was complaining about His work!

Another thing to consider is this: if you feed your brain negative thoughts long enough, you will begin to believe the negative things you are saying about yourself.

So instead of complaining about yourself, celebrate!

Your body is a terrific combination of talents, wisdom, knowledge and understanding. Rejoice in being you. Include yourself on your hero list.

✝ SCRIPTURE:

"So God created man in His own image...God saw all that He had made, and it was very good...." Genesis 1:27, 31

REFLECTION:

1) Do you put yourself down? Why or why not?

2) Do you know people who put themselves down? If so, what can you do to help these persons?

᠙ᢒ

✔ CHALLENGE:

Think of yourself as a hero today by making a list of the heroes in your life.

• Now take a look at your list. Did you include yourself?

• If you didn't, write your name on the list!

Feelings

Feelings Aren't Sins

Angry. Sad. Down-hearted. Feeling blue.

"Everyone experiences these feelings from time to time," says a Christian psychiatrist.

When I was a teen, I thought Christians should always be happy—no matter what. That is unrealistic. Jesus Christ didn't promise us that we wouldn't have problems on this earth.

No way!

The Bible says there will be times when we feel unhappy. Our salvation makes it certain that we won't be unhappy forever.

The sad feelings will pass.

That's not easy to remember when we're in the middle of the struggle. Find encouragement and strength in knowing that Christ cares about you and the struggles you have to confront.

"Don't keep your sad feelings bottled up inside," the Christian psychiatrist went on to say. "Bottled up feelings can lead to ulcers, heart attacks and a number of other diseases.

"Remember, Jesus experienced sadness, depression and anger too."

Share your feelings, the negative ones as well as positive, with other Christian friends. That's what the Christian church is for—sharing and encouraging one another.

✝ SCRIPTURE:

"There is a time for everything, and a season for every activity under heaven:...a time to weep and a time to laugh; a time to mourn and a time to dance..." Ecclesiastes 3:1,4

REFLECTION:

1) When you get blue, do you feel guilty? As a Christian, do you feel that you should constantly wear a smiling face?

2) Do you keep your sad feelings bottled up inside?

✿

✔ CHALLENGE:

The next time you're blue, try one or more of our blue-mood busters:

• Listen to your favorite song.

• Daydream about the happiest moment you've ever known, recalling sharp, vivid details of your happy memory to relive the pleasing experience.

• Read an enjoyable book.

Hurts

You are going to face hurts throughout your life. The Bible says that from time to time you will be faced with disappointments—even though you are a Christian.

There will be times when you don't get that good grade you wanted on your French test. Or algebra. Or history.

There will be times when you don't get that date with Bill. Or Mike. Or Kevin.

There will be times when your parents get on your case for not keeping your room neater. Or for not getting your chores done on time. Or for not helping with the yard work.

So why be a Christian?

Answer: Because the Bible promises God is always with us. Take a look at Matthew 28:20 where it says "...And surely I am with you always, to the very end of the age."

Notice the verse does not say God is with us only when we are happy. Or when we do good things. Or when we get good grades. The verse says always. That means during the hurting times too.

✝ SCRIPTURE:

"So do not fear, for I am with you; do not be dismayed, for I am your God. I will strengthen you and help you; I will uphold you with my righteous right hand." Isaiah 41:10

REFLECTION:

1) When was the last time you hurt? Recall how God helped you during that time.

2) What can you do when you face disappointment and struggles in your life?

✔ SUGGESTIONS:

The next time you hurt, try one or more of the following suggestions.

• Share your hurt with a Christian friend you trust. Talking to a friend can help.

• Remind yourself of this: Jesus Christ had hurting times, too.

• Medicate yourself—with God's word—while remembering the hurting time will pass. You won't always hurt.

Contentment

Times when everything goes right are such fun.

It's great to be voted the most popular and likeable person in class. It's totally awesome to be chosen class queen. It's wonderful to win a grand prize.

But what about those times when things don't go right?

It's not easy to be content when your parents are bugging you (again!) or when you fail a history test (after you studied for it!) or when your sister informs you that her closet is off limits (when you planned on borrowing a dress for the party Saturday night). At times like that, you probably feel like, "what's the use?"

That's a far cry from contentment.

Ask God to help you practice contentment in your life—whatever the circumstances may be. This is what the Bible instructs. Philippians 4:4-7 says: "Rejoice in the Lord always. I will say it again: Rejoice! Let your gentleness be evident to all. The Lord is near. Do not be anxious about anything, but in everything, by prayer and petition, with thanksgiving, present your requests to God. And the peace of God, which transcends all understanding, will guard your hearts and your minds in Christ Jesus."

✝ SCRIPTURE:

"I am not saying this because I am in need, for I have learned to be content whatever the circumstances." Philippians 4:11

REFLECTION:

1) Are you content today? Why or why not?

2) How can you find contentment when things don't go your way?

☙

✔ CHALLENGE:

To experience more contentment in your life, develop a hobby. Hobbies are great to develop skills and occupy the mind. Think of all the hobbies available that you may choose from:

- Gourmet cooking
- Reading
- Painting
- Singing
- Knitting
- Tennis
- Computers

The possibilities are endless!

Friendship

Selecting Friends

Take a moment to think about your friends.

Why are they your friends? Are they fun to be around? Do they encourage you? When you have a problem, do you look forward to sharing it with them?

If you've answered yes to these questions, you have some real friendships.

If you answered one or two questions with a firm no, evaluate your friends. Are they trying to get you to do things you really don't want to do, things you know are not Christian actions? If so, search for some true Christian friends who will allow you to live a Christian life as God intended.

Malinda and Ann are two high school juniors who have been friends since elementary school.

"I like Malinda because she never laughs or pokes fun at me," Ann says.

"I like Ann because she's always there for me when I have a problem," Malinda says.

Friends are great support.

Jesus said a lot about friends. In John 15:12-14 Jesus says, "My command is this: Love each other as I have loved you. Greater love has no one than this, that he lay down his life for his friends. You are my friends if you do what I command."

Besides selecting Christian friends for a nice support group for yourself, try to be a good friend, too.

✝ SCRIPTURE:

"A friend loves at all times,..." Proverbs 17:17

REFLECTION:

1) Thank God for your friends.

2) Reach out to develop friendships.

❧

✔ CHALLENGE:

Do one of the following today with a friend:

• Share feelings over a big bowl of buttered popcorn.

• Take a walk together in a nearby park or other scenic spot.

• Tell each other jokes.

• Enjoy a movie together.

Promises, Promises, and More Promises

Did you ever have a friend promise you something and then not keep the promise?

It happens to all of us. If you're honest, you will remember a promise, or several, you made to someone and then broke it.

All of us have broken promises at one time or another.

But God is different. He never breaks a promise. And the Bible is stuffed with promises. Just think of it. What a gift!

Listen to some of God's promises:

"You will call and I will answer you; you will long for the creature your hands have made." Job 14:15

"Peace I leave with you; my peace I give you. I do not give to you as the world gives. Do not let your hearts be troubled and do not be afraid." John 14:27

"Your sun will never set again, and your moon will wane no more; the Lord will be your everlasting light, and your days of sorrow will end." Isaiah 60:20

"For whoever wants to save his life will lose it, but whoever loses his life for me and for the gospel will save it." Mark 8:35

"As far as the east is from the west, so far has he removed our transgressions from us." Psalm 103:12

God specializes in promises. That's why when I feel blue or sad, I like to go through the Bible and read some promises. It always makes me feel better. Try it yourself—and be blessed!

✝ SCRIPTURE:

"As for God, his way is perfect; the word of the Lord is flawless. He is a shield for all who take refuge in him." 2 Samuel 22:31

ℰ

REFLECTION:

1) Think of one Bible promise that has meant a lot to you. Why has it meant so much?

2) Think of some of your favorite verses. See how many of them contain God's promises.

ℰ

✔ CHALLENGE:

• Witness your Christian life to a friend by sharing a Bible promise.

• Tell your friend what the promise means to you personally.

• Ask your friend if she has a Bible promise to share with you.

• Sharing Bible promises encourages Christian growth and fellowship with one another.

Me Forgive Me?

Is it hard for you to forgive a friend who hurts you? Sure, it probably is. But chances are that as a Christian, you have a nice habit of practicing forgiveness in your life when others hurt you.

But how about yourself? Do you ever forgive yourself?

It may sound like a crazy question until you think about it. To really feel good inside, you need to like yourself. To like yourself, you're going to have to forgive yourself—over and over again—whenever you make mistakes.

I used to think if I were a real Christian, I wouldn't do the things that needed forgiveness on my part. But later I learned that's not realistic. Romans 3:23-24 says, "For all have sinned and fall short of the glory of God, and are justified freely by his grace through the redemption that came by Christ Jesus."

Just because we're Christians doesn't mean we won't goof up, that we won't do things that will hurt us. When that happens, forgive yourself.

Don't fret.

Forget the past and go on.

That's what God wants you to do.

It's a beautiful feeling to forgive yourself. You will feel cleansed, refreshed and clean inside. And isn't that what Christianity is all about?

✝ SCRIPTURE:

"Be kind and compassionate to one another, forgiving each other, just as in Christ God forgave you." Ephesians 4:32

REFLECTION:

1) Make a list of the things you like about yourself. Don't be modest. There's a lot of good in everyone.

2) Now make a list of some of the things you don't like about yourself. Think of ways you can change.

ℰᴅ

✔ CHALLENGE:

Think about something you've done that you have not forgiven yourself for. Take the time to forgive yourself now. How? Simply pray the Lord's Prayer, which includes the asking of forgiveness. "Forgive us our sins, for we also forgive everyone who sins against us..." Luke 11: 4

Look on the Bright Side

Bright Side

No doubt you're familiar with the example of a glass half filled with water. Would you say the glass was half full or half empty?

There are two sides to everything—a bright side (half full) and a dull side (half empty).

Which side do you focus on?

As a Christian, you can focus on the bright side. Life is more productive and joyous that way.

And the choice is yours.

Some people choose to be optimistic while others choose to be pessimistic. For example, I knew two waitresses, named Julie and Pat, who worked in a restaurant. Every day when they came to work, Julie would talk about what a nice day it was while Pat complained about the weather.

"Oh, the sun feels so good," Julie said one day after arriving at work.

Pat frowned. "But it's so hot!"

A steady customer overheard the conversation and asked: "Why do the two of you always see the weather so differently? We've been having nice weather."

"But it is hot!" Pat insisted, even though the temperature was in the seventies. "But there's a cool breeze. It's so refreshing!" Julie said.

Notice how Julie chose to focus on the bright side. It's no wonder others liked to be with Julie more than Pat.

People feel drained when they are around people like Pat. But people enjoy being around others with a positive outlook—like Julie.

If you want to focus on the positive, try reading Psalms 119:57-72 sometime. Notice when David began writing the Psalms he was depressed. But through the grace of God, he learned how to focus on the bright side. David says in verse 71 that he was actually grateful he was afflicted!

Sometimes we can even be grateful during sad times. We can be glad that God is with us and ask him to help us see a brighter side.

✝ SCRIPTURE:

"Give thanks to the Lord, for he is good; his love endures forever." Psalms 118:1

REFLECTION:

1) Are you a person who concentrates on the joyful things in life? Or are you a person who sees only the negative side of things?

2) What can you do to develop a positive attitude?

✔ CHALLENGE:

Concentrate on the positive side of life by doing one or more of the following:

• Pick a bowl of wild flowers and *see* their beauty.

• Enjoy others by saying hello and smiling at everyone you see today.

• Look for the good qualities in people and overlook the not-so-good things.

Is Your Life One Total Maze?

Do you feel caught up in an uncertain future, not knowing if you will be successful—at getting into college, making friends, or getting a certain guy to like you? Does your path to the future seem like one hopeless, complicated maze?

If you feel you don't know where your future is leading you, be assured these feelings are normal for teen girls.

Find comfort in the fact that Christ dwells in you. He will lead you to successful Christian living—if you let Him. Welcome Him in your daily life. When the future seems frightening, ask God to direct you. Absorb His rich goodness, strength, peace and blessings.

Learn to trust God. How? Ask God to help you not to worry about tomorrow. Concentrate on today.

Reflect on these verses from Matthew 6:25-26. "Therefore I tell you, do not worry about your life, what you will eat or drink; or about your body, what you will wear. Is not life more important than food, and the body more important than clothes? Look at the birds of the air; they do not sow or reap or store away in barns, and yet your heavenly Father feeds them."

† SCRIPTURE:

"Trust in the Lord with all your heart and lean not on your own understanding; in all your ways acknowledge him, and he will make your paths straight." Proverbs 3:5,6

REFLECTION:

1) What can we do to stop worrying about the future?

2) How can we trust God?

ço

✔CHALLENGE:

Worrying about tomorrow is habit forming. Try to develop a habit *not* to worry about tomorrow:

• Copy down today's scriptures on note cards and carry them in your purse.

• The next time you begin worrying about tomorrow, read the cards and reflect on the comforting verses to remind yourself that God will take care of you.

Change

Change can be exciting or frightening.

For instance, isn't it fun to change your weekend plans after a guy calls for a date? On the other hand, isn't it disappointing to have to change your class schedule after you discover your favorite class is full?

Whether change is exciting or frightening, one thing is certain. You will have to deal with change throughout your life.

Change will surround you.

Sometimes you may make plans to go to a friend's house and have to stay home instead because you are sick with a fever.

Other times you may have a picnic planned when it rains and so you have to eat indoors. Or perhaps out of the clear blue your parents move to a different city.

Some people try to avoid change in their lives and, as a result, end up with a lot of misery. Others confront change positively and use it for beautiful spiritual growth.

Alcoholics Anonymous is noted for the serenity prayer that features change. Perhaps you've heard the prayer or even said it yourself.

If you're not familiar with the prayer, it goes like this:

Lord, grant me the serenity to accept the things I cannot change, courage to change the things I can, and wisdom to know the difference. Memorize this prayer and say it—it works.

That way you can adjust to the changes in your life accordingly. Sometimes the changes will be difficult. Pray that God will help you deal with the changes in your life constructively so that you may grow spiritually from change.

Note the Bible verse below that says we can ask God for such things.

✝ SCRIPTURE:

"Ask and it will be given to you; seek and you will find; knock and the door will be opened to you. For everyone who asks receives; he who seeks finds; and to him who knocks, the door will be opened." Matthew 7:7,8

ℰઝ

REFLECTION:

1) Review some of the recent changes you had in your life. How did you handle them? With hope? Or fear?

2) Why do we have to learn to cope with change?

ℰઝ

✔ CHALLENGE:

Test your change adaptability factor:

Suppose your school principal announces the school cafeteria will be closed for repairs. Do you panic and tell your mother the school officials are starving you to death? Or do you see this as an opportunity to pack yourself a tasty sack lunch?

I'm sure you can see the last answer is a more positive way to respond.

Pray the serenity prayer sometime today.

Let's Have Fun!

Can Christians Have Fun ?

Have you ever wondered if Christians can have fun? I know I did when I was a teen. It seemed like all I ever heard from grown-ups was what Christians should *not* do.

"Don't go too far with a boy."

"Don't drink." "Don't do drugs." "Don't smoke." "Don't swear."

The list goes on and on. At times I felt like I was doomed for a life of gloom. But as I read my Bible, I found some surprises.

I learned Christians had lots of fun in Biblical times. In Deuteronomy 16, it says that people held a festival at harvest time. Verse 15 says, "For seven days celebrate the Feast to the Lord your God at the place the Lord will choose. For the Lord your God will bless you in all your harvest and in all the work of your hands, and your joy will be complete."

And Numbers, chapter 21, says Christians rejoiced when water was discovered. Verse 17 says: "Then Israel sang this song: 'Spring up, Oh well! Sing about it...'"

And notice in Psalm, chapter 92, Biblical people praised the Lord for the Sabbath celebration. Try reading these scriptures for more details.

Today Christians still have fun. Look at the Christians you know. See how they celebrate Sunday and everyday life. And doesn't it make sense when you stop and think about it? If Christians can't have fun, who can?

So enjoy life by having fun with God. He loves to have fun with you!

✝ SCRIPTURE:

"For you make me glad by your deeds, O Lord; I sing for joy at the works of your hands." Psalms 92:4

✌

REFLECTION:

1) Are you having fun with God? If you're not, why not?

2) Study the Christians you know and observe the fun they have with God.

✌

✔ CHALLENGE:

Have some fun by following one or more of our fun-filled ideas:

• Throw a come-as-you-are party.

• Go to youth group this coming Sunday evening.

• Join the church choir.

• Learn to play an instrument.

• Try a new hobby. If you don't like it, try another... and another...until you find one you enjoy.

Drugs Aren't Funny...or Fun!

When writer-comedian Erma Bombeck was on a talk show recently, a woman from the audience asked:

"Erma, why don't you ever have anything funny about drugs in your jokes?" Erma stopped smiling, nodded soberly, and answered: "To me, drugs aren't funny."

The audience applauded.

They agreed.

Drugs aren't funny...or fun!

That may not be what your friends tell you. They may say it's fun to take drugs. You may even have tried some coke—or speed—or alcohol. Maybe you did reach a high. Don't let that high fool you. Drugs won't do one good thing for you. After the highs, come lows...depression, anxiety, fear, panic.

Sure, you may be tempted to try drugs. Or, if you've already experimented with drugs, you may want to keep right on experimenting.

The Bible doesn't promise us a life free of temptation. Quite the contrary. The Bible does, however, say in I Corinthians 10:13 that God provides escapes from temptation. It says, "No temptation has seized you except what is common to man. And God is faithful; he will not let you be tempted beyond what you can bear. But when you are tempted, he will also provide a way out so that you can stand up under it."

Study this verse and think about it to keep straight.

† SCRIPTURE:

"Lead me, O Lord, in your righteousness because of my enemies—make straight your way before me."
Psalms 5:8

REFLECTION:

1. Have you ever wanted to take drugs? Or have you tried drugs already?

2. Do you know someone who is presently on drugs? If so, how would you describe that person? Happy? Sad? Frightened? Confused? Wearing a "mask" a lot of the time to protect inner feelings from showing?

ℰℬ

✔ CHALLENGE:

Try one or more of the "escapes" listed below the next time you're tempted to do drugs. (These escapes have actually been used successfully by recovering women drug addicts when they were tempted to have a drink of alcohol or use some other kind of drug.)

• Take a long, warm, relaxing bubble bath with suds filled to the top of the tub.

• Call a friend and talk about your temptation.

• Make yourself a frozen, nutritious and drug-free drink by mixing together: 1/3 cup orange juice, 1/3 cup milk, 1 teaspoon vanilla and 1/2 cup crushed ice.

Day by Day...

Daydreaming

It's a gorgeous spring day. The school windows are open.

A cool, gentle breeze sweeps across my face. I study the robin in the maple tree nearby. Maybe after school, Marilyn and I can go on a picnic. I remember Mom has some leftover fried chicken in the refrigerator...

"What does our lesson say?" the teacher is asking me.

I jump to reality. How do I know what the lesson says? I was daydreaming!

It can be quite embarrassing if the teacher calls on you for an answer when your mind is several planets away. Your classmates' giggles are anything but music to your ears.

But daydreaming in the right place and time is great.

Outstanding inventions, exciting books and new products come from people who took the time to daydream.

At home, curl up on your bed or in a favorite chair and take time to daydream. Just let your imagination take you to some of your favorite scenic spots. Visualize quiet wooded forests or the mysterious rhythm of ocean waves to get in a relaxed mood.

Or dream about the future. Think of what you want to do and imagine yourself ten or twenty years from now, engaged in the occupation you would like.

Isn't it fun to daydream?

God gave you a special gift when he gave you a mind that can take you to faraway and imaginative places. Use it daily.

✝ SCRIPTURE:

"A heart at peace gives life to the body, but envy rots the bones." Proverbs 14:30

REFLECTION:

1) Do you have a habit of daydreaming? Or are you usually too rushed to take the time?

2) Set aside some time—five, ten, twenty minutes or more—to daydream every day.

✔ CHALLENGE:

Today, daydream and do something constructive with your daydreams. For example:

• Draw or paint a picture of the scenic spot you daydream about.

• Be creative! Write a story using your daydreams for the plot.

• Call a friend and share your daydream with her.

Now

You want to develop better study habits—and you will, you think, starting next week... after the weekend.

You want to lose a few excess pounds—and you will, you promise, starting tomorrow...after dinner (and dessert).

You want to visit that pleasant elderly couple from church—and you will, you think,...in a couple of weeks, after you get organized.

Procrastination.

It happens to all of us at one time or another, but don't let it become a habit. It's a *bad* habit.

Now is the time to do the things you want to do. Take action to do those things—now—today. Never depend on tomorrow. Tomorrow is a cop-out. It never comes.

Failure is often the result of procrastination. For example, a junior high student kept saying she would study for her science test. Later.

I'm sure you can guess what happened. Later never came. The student failed the test—not because she wasn't smart but because she failed to study.

You can learn from her mistake. No doubt you've had a similar experience. Remember not to put things off until tomorrow.

† SCRIPTURE:

"I tell you, now is the time of God's favor, now is the day of salvation." II Corinthians 6:2b

REFLECTION:

1) When was the last time you procrastinated about something? What happened?

2) What are you putting off in your life right now that you really need to do?

જી

✔ CHALLENGE:

Write a list of what you need to do today. Then treat yourself after you get everything done! You will feel good—and you have every reason to—about getting your work accomplished.

Excited About Your Future Career?

"What do you want to be in your adult life?"

That's the question you will hear throughout your teen years. When you answer it, observe your voice. Does it sound excited? Do you feel excited inside? Or do you answer gloomily, without enthusiasm and with sagging shoulders?

A high school guidance counselor said he could tell if a student made a good career choice by the way the student answered that particular question.

"If their eyes light up and the student acts excited, I know that student has made a good career choice," the counselor explained. "But if a student hesitates, lowers his head and mumbles the answer, that student probably needs some counseling about his career."

Get excited about your future career.

Reach—and strive—for what you want out of life. Take an inward journey to discover what you want to be. Dare to dream big. Big accomplishments come from big dreams.

"But people may laugh if I tell them I want to be a medical doctor," you may tell yourself.

Suppose they laugh. So what? God won't laugh. Remember that God knows your sincerity as you make your career choice.

Ask God to direct you. Ask for His wisdom to chose a career that excites you and will glorify Him.

† SCRIPTURE:

"As for God, his way is perfect; the word of the Lord is flawless. He is a shield for all who take refuge in him." 2 Samuel 22:31

REFLECTION:

1) Have you decided on a career? If you have, are you excited about it? If you aren't, why aren't you?

2) Have you asked God to direct your path to choose the right career?

֍

✔ CHALLENGE:

Plan your future by:

• Talking to some of your teachers about your career and listening to their advice.

• Reading library books about the different careers you want to consider.

• Studying college catalogs to see what courses are available.

• Talking to someone in that career. Ask questions.

Treating Yourself

What do you like to do? Listen to music? Read a good book? Take a walk in a wooded park? Curl up on your friend's bed and just talk?

Every teen girl needs to treat herself. Treats are a spiritual refreshment, a time of relaxation and pure enjoyment of living.

We often confuse money with treats. We think it takes money to treat ourselves. But stop and take another look at the treats named above. None of them cost anything.

If you aren't enjoying any treats in life, you can change. Simply take the time to treat yourself. Stop and read that novel you've been wanting to for so long. Take time to have a Pepsi with your girl friend. Give yourself time to take a jog through the woods. Treat *yourself*. No one else can do it for you.

✝ SCRIPTURE:

"Come, let us sing for joy to the Lord; let us shout aloud to the Rock of our salvation. Let us come before him with thanksgiving and extol him with music and song." Psalms 95:1-2

REFLECTION:

1) When was the last time you treated yourself? (Don't count anything that cost money, such as buying a new dress).

2) Why are treats important in the Christian life?

✔ CHALLENGE:

Take some time today from your schedule to treat yourself by doing one or more of the following:

• Invite a friend over and have her give you a new hair style.

• Go for a jog; exercise is a great way to treat your body.

• Pop some popcorn and enjoy a television movie.

• Give your mind a free vacation—curl up on your bed, close your eyes and daydream about the sound of ocean waves or visualize a bright green forest.

• Relax with a good book.

Beauty...Inside or Out?...Or Both?

Getting Beautiful

Beauty.

What is it?

A pretty movie star?

Most people think of physical attractiveness when they think of beauty. You are probably no exception. After all, make-up is fun. Experimenting with lip glosses, eye shadow and mascara is generally a part of every teen girl's world.

But don't get so hung up on make-up that you forget about inner beauty, true beauty.

Take a sincere look at yourself. Are you easy-going or do you fly off the handle over trivial things? Do you take time to be a blessing to others? Or are you concerned mostly with yourself and what pleases you? Do you reach out and take risks to develop friendships or do you keep to yourself to play it safe?

Ask God to help direct you to develop a fully beautiful woman inside.

Smiles, a joyful disposition, a positive outlook on life and caring for others are the tools to attain inner Christian beauty.

† SCRIPTURE:

"Your beauty should not come from outward adornment, such as braided hair and the wearing of gold jewelry and fine clothes. Instead, it should be that of your inner self, the unfading beauty of a gentle and quiet spirit, which is of great worth in God's sight." I Peter 3:3,4

REFLECTION:

1) Are you spending too much time on your outside beauty and not enough on inner beauty? Only you and God can answer that.

2) If your answer was yes, what can you do to change?

❧

CHALLENGE:

• Grab a piece of paper and write down all the things you like about your inward beauty (such as being kind to others, etc.). No doubt there are a lot of good things in your inner make up.

• After you write the list, look it over—and feel good about yourself.

Self-Esteem

Self-esteem is vital to living a Christian life.

After all, how can we help others if we don't value ourselves first? We can't.

"But I can't do anything!" you may say. "I have no talents of my own." Or probably you think you look terrible, that you will never get rid of your "zits."

Or perhaps you feel that no one likes you.

Well, we aren't perfect, but God accepts us and loves us just the way we are. He loves you so very much that He sent His son to die just for you. I admit sometimes that's hard for me to comprehend, but I always find comfort in reminding myself of how Jesus suffered the crucifixion just for me.

Take time today to remind yourself that Jesus Christ died on the cross for you and he rose again...for you. After a few minutes, you'll feel your self-esteem rising.

No matter what negative thoughts you have in your life right now, get rid of them. Remember, God created us in His image. That means you are good because you are part of God!

Feed that positive, miraculous, true thought into your brain and find yourself feeling great. Feel your self-esteem thermometer rise. Rejoice that you are one of God's special, unrepeatable miracles—a very precious miracle that God values.

Only you can choose what you want for your life. Choose positive things under God's direction. And reach out to help others. Volunteer work is a great way to feel good about yourself while living the Christian life.

† SCRIPTURE:

"Then God said, `Let us make man in our image, in our likeness, and let them rule over the fish of the sea and the birds of the air, over the livestock, over all the earth, and over all the creatures that move along the ground.'" Genesis 1:26

ᏀᎧ

REFLECTION:

1) Why should you love and accept yourself?

2) How can you feel good about yourself?

ᏀᎧ

✔ CHALLENGES:

Sign up for some volunteer work. For example you could:

• Be a volunteer at a hospital.

• Serve as a kindergarten aide for the Sunday School teacher.

• Do something constructive at a nursing home— like playing the piano to entertain the residents or reading a book to one or several of the residents.

• Help tutor younger children.

Special Gifts

Did you know you have at least one special gift and perhaps several?

"Aw, I can't do anything," you may moan.

But you can. Think about what you like to do. Maybe God gave you a lovely singing voice. Or a talent for drawing. Or perhaps the good Lord blessed you with a love for taking care of children.

Discover your gift—or gifts—if you haven't already. Then use the gifts for God's glory.

Sometimes grown-ups let their gifts fade away or they never develop them. This is sad.

God gave us gifts so we could use them for others. What good, for instance, is a lovely singing voice if no one ever hears it? Does it matter if you have a talent for drawing when you don't draw for other people to see your work? Or why have a talent for taking care of children if you never volunteer in the church nursery?

Treasure your gift.

"But," you may say, "I don't know what I'm good at."

That's fine. Ask God to help you discover what you're good at. Observe the things you do well. Then develop and use your talent. Let other people benefit from your talent.

† SCRIPTURE:

"There are different kinds of gifts, but the same Spirit. There are different kinds of service, but the same Lord. There are different kinds of working, but the same God works all of them in all men. Now to each one the manifestation of the Spirit is given for the common good." 1 Corinthians 12:4-7

REFLECTION:

    1) What is your special gift or gifts?

    2) Are you developing your talents?

ℱℨ

✔ CHALLENGE:

Think of some girls you know who have developed their gifts.

• For example, do you know someone who plays well in the band?

• Or a girl who bakes the best chocolate chip cookies?

• Or maybe you know someone who seems to always know what to say around elderly people or in awkward situations.

• Make it a point to tell the girls that you've noticed their gifts. Let them know their gifts have been a blessing to you.

Dating...and Some Controversial Issues

How Can I Get a Date?

Does God care about my date life?

I heard a young person ask that question in an adult Sunday School class.

You may be interested—and pleased!—to know all of the adults gave an immediate response: yes, of course He does!

Sometimes it seems silly to teens to even attempt incorporating dating problems into their prayer life. But it's not. Dating is or will be a most important area in your life.

When was the last time you talked to God about your date life? Or have you ever talked to Him about it? If you're longing for a nice date with a Christian guy, by all means, pray about it. God believes in romance.

Wanting to eventually marry is part of nearly every teen girl's dreams. And that's what God intended.

So don't be embarrassed or afraid to talk to God about your date life. Pray about making the right decisions when dating. Learn what God wants for you when it comes to guys.

Note the following Bible verse tells how God intends for people to marry and have a loving relationship.

✝ SCRIPTURE:

"For this reason a man will leave his father and mother and be united to his wife, and they will become one flesh." Genesis 2:24

ℒ

REFLECTION:

1) What difference might there be if I prayed about my date life?

2) Talk to your parents or other adults about how God helped them in dating.

✔ SUGGESTION:

Take some time today to ask God for His blessing and guidance for your date life by praying a simple prayer:

Dear God, would you please bless me in my date life? Show me the way to meet nice guys. Help me to have Christian fun with them. Amen.

Love ...Is It Money?

What exactly is love?

Consider this story.

Kyle and Amy had been going steady for three months during their sophomore high school year.

"I'm going to ask Kyle to take me to an expensive restaurant for dinner Saturday," Amy told her best friend, Malinda. "He'll do it if he loves me."

"Doesn't that depend on more than love?" Malinda wanted to know.

Amy perched an eyebrow. "What do you mean?"

"I mean maybe Kyle doesn't have the money," Malinda said realistically.

"Nonsense!" Amy shrugged. "That's my point, Malinda. If he loves me, he'll do it."

But it turned out Malinda was right. Kyle couldn't afford an expensive restaurant for the two of them, but Amy did not understand. She broke off the relationship.

The scripture verses below make an excellent guide for your dating life.

✝ SCRIPTURE:

"Love is patient, love is kind. It does not envy, it does not boast, it is not proud. It is not rude, it is not self-seeking, it is not easily angered, it keeps not record of wrongs." I Corinthians 13:4, 5

🙜

REFLECTION:

1) Was Amy justified in her actions of expecting Kyle to buy her an expensive dinner?

2) Should money be of great importance in our lives?

❦

✔ CHALLENGE:

Incorporate Christian love into your relationships by trying one of our challenges sometime:

• Suggest going on a picnic date instead of to a restaurant. Then offer to provide part of the food for the event.

• Invite your date to a fun-filled—and free!—church youth group event.

Guys and Sex

If you flipped to this page first before you started reading any other meditations, don't be embarrassed. Your curious feelings about the opposite sex are normal.

"But what do I do with those feelings?" you may wonder.

You probably didn't notice guys in your preteen years. But then all of a sudden you woke up one day and saw guys.

They were handsome! When did they get that way? you wonder. Why didn't you notice guys before now?

Teens develop a strong interest in the opposite sex. Even though that interest is exciting, it can create problems if not controlled.

The Bible says a lot about sex. In I Thessalonians 4:3-8, it says, "It is God's will that you should be sanctified: that you should avoid sexual immorality; that each of you should learn to control his own body in a way that is holy and honorable, not in passionate lust like the heathen, who do not know God..."

How do you apply the scripture to your life? What if you really love a guy? What's wrong with sex then?

"If you really love me, you'd do it with me," he says. "If you really love me, you wouldn't try to make me do something I don't want to do," you reply!

Consider this. Every year thousands of teen girls become pregnant.

"But I'm mature," you may argue. "I know about birth control."

So did 17-year-old Malissa. She became pregnant anyway. It happens. The most common forms of birth control are more failure-prone than kids think. Malissa almost got an abortion. But after much prayer, she decided to have the baby—and keep it.

"It wasn't an easy decision," she admits. "And it's not fun to raise a baby when you're still a teen yourself. Babies are a lot more than pink bundles of cuteness. They scream at night for feedings, fuss often during the day and are expensive to feed and clothe."

Would you be willing to sacrifice your teen years as Malissa is doing—for single motherhood? It's something to think about.

Sex is a precious God-given gift. When you save sex for marriage, lots of problems can be avoided. Make this your policy: "I'm being faithful to the husband I haven't met yet!"

✝ SCRIPTURE:

"Flee from sexual immorality. All other sins a man commits are outside his body, but he who sins sexually sins against his own body. Do you not know that your body is a temple of the Holy Spirit, who is in you, whom you have received from God? You are not your own; you were bought at a price. Therefore honour God with your body." I Corinthians 6:18-20

ℰ

REFLECTION:

1) Is your physical attraction for guys normal?

2) What does the Bible suggest you do with your strong feelings for guys and sex?

ℰ

✔ CHALLENGE:

Do you know a teen-age girl who is pregnant? If so, be kind to her and extend yourself to her in friendship.

Saying No Can Be Beautiful

"If you love me, you'll let me have sex with you."

Teen girls tell me that's a popular line with guys today. Teen girls also say they often don't know how to respond to that statement.

Sixteen-year-old Amy says she really does love her boyfriend Mike but she wants to save lovemaking for marriage.

"I know that seems old-fashioned in this day and age," she said recently. "And I've been laughed at, too, by other girls, but I want to stand up for my rights. I told Mike no, I wanted to save sex for marriage. We both want to go to college first. And you know what? I thought he would laugh. But he says he loves me more for saying no."

In a recent newspaper column by Ann Landers, a high school sophomore girl had a similar experience. She wrote Ann to say she was glad she said no to a guy who asked her to have sex.

"It would have been easy to give in, but I decided not to let him take advantage of me," the girl wrote. "It took guts to fight, but I feel good about asserting myself."

The girl went on to say she hoped her letter would give other teen girls courage to do the same thing. No doubt it will.

Isn't it wonderful when other Christians share their struggles—and victories—when turning to God?

Ann Landers, you may be interested to know, responded by saying that "no" is a beautiful and important word in a girl's vocabulary.

"It can mean the difference between a joyous future and a miserable one," Ann wrote. "It can also mean respect, confidence and peace of mind."

✝ SCRIPTURE:

"(Love) is not rude, it is not self-seeking, it is not easily angered, it keeps no record of wrongs. Love does not delight in evil but rejoices with the truth." I Corinthians 13:5, 6

⳨

REFLECTION:

1) What can you tell a guy if he says he wants sex with you before marriage?

2) Think about how you want to feel when you get married. Do you want that sex to be new and special?

⳨

✔ CHALLENGE:

Develop some Christian views on sex by:

• Talking to your parents about sex and marriage.

• Talking to God about sex and marriage in your prayer life.

• Reading Christian books, including the Bible, on relationships.

Abortion

Abortion is a critical—and controversial—issue today. Every year millions of women, for various reasons, decide to abort unborn babies.

Maybe you know someone who has had an abortion. Or maybe you've even had an abortion yourself.

After Susan, 16, had an abortion, she couldn't put it out of her mind.

"I'm terribly sorry," Susan cried. "I'm not sure I did the right thing. Will God ever forgive me?"

The answer for Christians is yes, of course. God is loving and compassionate with those who sincerely want His forgiveness. There's no way He is going to condemn every woman who gets an abortion. If you are in your teens and have had the tragic crisis of having an abortion and can't experience God's forgiveness, think about this:

We know that God's mercy extends to all created beings, even to those who did not have an opportunity to live.

In claiming God's promise of forgiveness, don't forget to forgive yourself. Pray for strength and courage for present and future living.

Susan today is married—with two children. She knows she is forgiven. Isn't God great?

✝SCRIPTURE:

"For God so loved the world that he gave his one and only Son, that whoever believes in him shall not perish but have eternal life. For God did not send his Son into the world to condemn the world, but to save the world through him." John 3:16-17

REFLECTION:

1) What does the Bible say about judging others? (Luke 6:27-38)

2) Think of ways not to judge others in your life.

❦

✔ CHALLENGE:

Abortion is such a serious issue today. You can be a Christian witness to other girls by:

• Saving sexual activity for your husband.

• Refraining from playing God in judging girls who have had an abortion.

• Talking to your Mom (or another woman you respect) about developing a Christian life-style in sexual matters.

• Taking a personal stand, based on the Bible, regarding your own actions and attitudes.

Homosexuality

Surely homosexuality is another one of the most controversial issues in today's society. Some say it's wrong and that a homosexual can be changed to heterosexual. Others say there's nothing wrong with homosexuality and that a person is born with homosexual genes. Scientifically, the jury is still out on which origin prevails—nature or nurture.

Read what the Bible says on the subject. Homosexuality is nothing new. It existed in Biblical times, too.

In Romans 1:26-27 Paul says: "Because of this, God gave them over to shameful lusts. Even their women exchanged natural relations for unnatural ones. In the same way the men also abandoned natural relations with women and were inflamed with lust for one another. Men committed indecent acts with other men, and received in themselves the due penalty for their perversion."

The Bible says that sex between a man and a woman was developed partly for creating the family. That would push homosexuality out of the picture.

As you draw your conclusions, don't judge the homosexual. Even though the Bible consistently condemns this sin, it's not a sin that can't be forgiven. Remember God distinguishes between the sinner and the sin.

When Darcy went to college, she was surprised and didn't know what to do when a female colleague said she was in love with Darcy. The colleague made "sexual type" advances.

"I just stood there, staring at her," Darcy recalled. "I didn't know what to do. I was terribly afraid and didn't want to participate in anything homosexual."

Darcy recalls praying silently to God at the time.

After prayer, Darcy told the girl that she didn't want to be another woman's lover. In the process, Darcy found she had to forgive the girl for making advances. Result? The girls were friends, but not lovers.

Ask God for guidance in your sexual life. He can help.

After all, He's the one who invented sex.

†SCRIPTURE:

"Do you not know that the wicked will not inherit the kingdom of God? Do not be deceived: Neither the sexually immoral nor idolators nor adulterers nor male prostitutes nor homosexual offenders nor thieves nor the greedy nor drunkards nor slanderers nor swindlers will inherit the kingdom of God. And that is what some of you were. But you were washed, you were sanctified, you were justified in the name of the Lord Jesus Christ and by the Spirit of our God." I Corinthians 6:9-11

REFLECTION:

1) What does God say about homosexuality? What does God say about homosexuals?

2) What does being a Christian mean for how you treat homosexual persons?

✔ CHALLENGES:

Don't judge the homosexual. Instead reach out to him or her with the following Christ-like actions:

• If you're confident your Sunday School class or youth group will be compassionate, invite him or her to attend.

• Get the phone number of a Christian community group that offers counseling to homosexuals, in case you run into a situation where a homosexual would ask for help.

Parents!!!

Parents! Who Needs Them?

Let's be honest. Parents are difficult at times.

They complain when they hear loud music coming from your room. They won't let you go to a party unless an adult is there. And they think your boyfriend's hair is much too long.

It's not like you're a kid anymore, you figure! Can't they see that? If only, if only they'd get real!

Wait—time out.

Chances are your parents realize you're no longer a kid. And that's exactly why they seem overprotective. They want you to grow up to be a responsible Christian adult. But it surely doesn't seem that way to you. It seems more like war—a war they're determined to win.

It might help you to know that even Jesus had problems with his parents.

Recall the popular Bible story of 12-year-old Jesus talking to religious leaders in the temple. Jesus' parents were very upset when they had to look for him. And what was Jesus' reaction when his parents found him? In Luke 2:49, Jesus asks his mother, "Didn't you know I had to be in my Father's house?"

So, that's a fine story, but exactly how can you get along better with your parents in today's society? Take a look at the challenges on the next page. Try them. See if they work.

† SCRIPTURE:

"Then he went down to Nazareth with them and was obedient to them. But his mother treasured all these things in her heart." Luke 2:51

REFLECTION:

1) Are you the only one who can't get along with your parents?

2) What can you do when your parents get on your case?

✔ CHALLENGE:

To establish a good relationship with your parents:

• In a pleasant voice, ask them if they will listen to you.

• Tell your parents you will listen to them also. Be sure you do!

• When they voice concern about something you want, explain or show your parents the situation. For example: You want to rent a video and they're concerned about violence, sex or another issue that may be in the video. Ask if they'd be willing to view the movie first. Then accept their decision without argument. When children show consideration for their parents' feelings, the parents can develop trust and confidence in their children.

Demands

"If I don't get a new dress for the party, I'll just die."

"If Jerry doesn't ask me for a date to the church youth group banquet, I'll never go to church again."

"If I can't have a sleepover, I'll never clean my room again."

Demands.

Do you ever make them?

Sometimes people want something so much, they make ridiculous-sounding demands that are unfair.

Be careful when you want something too much.

"But how will I know if I want something too much?" you may ask.

Try listening to yourself. Are you making demands from other people? If you are, you want something too much. Take another look at the above examples. See how making demands isn't a Christian action.

So instead of insisting on getting your own way, take an inventory of yourself. Do you really need what you want? Or has your want become an unreasonable obsession?

Ask God to help you get rid of the demands in your life. Notice how the following Bible verse says God gives us all we need.

† SCRIPTURE:

"The Lord is my shepherd, I shall not be in want. He makes me lie down in green pastures, he leads me beside quiet waters, he restores my soul." Psalms 23:1,2

REFLECTION:

1) When was the last time you demanded something? What happened?

2) Has anyone ever demanded anything from you? If so, how did you feel about it? What happened?

✔ CHALLENGE:

• Avoid making demands in your daily Christian walk with the Lord by being grateful for what you have.

• Check off how many things from the following list that you have and can be grateful for:

- a warm home
- food and clothing
- friends and parents and other relatives
- Sunday School and public school teachers
- church youth leaders and ministers
- books and music
- hobby materials

• See how the list of things to be grateful for in our lives is endless.

Patience...Nice Word!

Patience.

It's a nice word. If only your parents could have a little more of it, you think. Sometimes you would like for your classmates to be more patient, too. And your impossible brat brother—now he could use a big dose of patience!

Hold it. Take a look at yourself. How patient are you?

Sure, you were hoping no one would check *your* patience.

It's easy to see when others need more patience, but it's harder to look honestly at yourself.

Naturally you can't change the way other people deal with situations. But you can change yourself. You can develop patience—with God's help.

"But why should I even try if my brother is a pest all the time anyway?" you may ask.

Answer: Because God wants you to be concerned about the patience in your life. How much patience others have is out of your control.

That means the next time you think your parents or classmates or brother should be more patient, try being more patient yourself. The Bible even tells us to wait patiently for the Lord Himself. In Psalms 37:7 it says: "Be still before the Lord and wait patiently for him..."

† SCRIPTURE:

"I know your deeds, your love and faith, your service and perseverance and that you are now doing more than you did at first." Revelation 2:19

REFLECTION:

1) Think of a time when you were patient. What were the results?

2) Think of a time when you weren't patient. What were the results?

❧

✔ CHALLENGE:

Be patient by implementing these challenges into your life.

• Stop being in a hurry (walk—don't run—to class).

• Before going home from school, take a couple moments to look over your notes to make sure you've got all of tomorrow's assignments.

• The next time you have to wait a few moments for someone, think of something pleasant while you wait.

Stress, Stress and More Stress!

Stress surrounds you.

Ever have your teacher ask you to turn in a book report—when you forgot to read a book? Imagine that the same day your p.e. teacher asks why you can't do a push up. And, on top of that, your mother wants to know when you're going to clean your room.

Why does everything have to land on your shoulders all at once? Can't anyone understand you're stressed to the max?

As Christians, we need to learn how to deal with the stress in our lives.

How?

By looking at how Jesus Christ dealt with stress. Just because He lived on earth nearly two thousand years ago, it doesn't mean He isn't a good role model today for teens.

He is.

Think of how Jesus was stressed during his ministering.

People rushed in crowds to Him. Some people wanted to be healed of a physical illness. Others wanted Jesus to teach them about God, our heavenly father, and the mysterious but beautiful Holy Spirit. Still others wanted Jesus to give them advice on how to live.

Sometimes Jesus got so stressed that He made it a point to get away from the crowds and went to a special place to pray. The Bible verse below illustrates such an example.

Think of ways you can do the same thing in your life when everyone gets on your case. Try going to your room the next time you're stressed. Flop on your bed with the Bible—and read about Jesus dealing with stress.

✝SCRIPTURE:

"Very early in the morning, while it was still dark, Jesus got up, left the house and went off to a solitary place, where he prayed." Mark 1:35

৪১

REFLECTION:

1) What stressed Jesus?

2) What stresses you?

৪১

✔CHALLENGES:

Try one or more of our stress-busters:
• Go for a swim.
• Call a friend over to visit.
• Play a computer game.
• Have a girlfriend rub your back.
• Tell a responsible Christian woman about some things that stress you. Listen to her advice.

Loneliness

Loneliness

Ever feel left out?

Like everyone has a life but you?

That things will never be okay in your world?

Loneliness is everything it's cracked up to be. All of the dismal things written about loneliness are true.

One day my friend asked, "What's worse than loneliness?"

I couldn't think of anything. It's terrible to feel so down, like no one cares.

And teen girls especially are plagued with lonely feelings from time to time. Maybe you felt lonely when you didn't make the cheerleading squad—or school band—or get that major role in the school play. Or perhaps everything was going fine in your life when all of a sudden—WHAM!—you felt all alone but you didn't know why.

Regardless of what your environment is at the time loneliness strikes, it's a yucky feeling.

So what can you, as a Christian teen girl, do when you get lonely? A couple of things.

First don't rely on money to prevent loneliness. It doesn't work! Instead, rely on God because He is always with you and will never let you down.

✝ Second, listen to the advice a minister gives his congregation: "Where the love of others leaves off, God's love continues." In Psalms 27:10 it says: "Though my father and my mother forsake me, the Lord will receive me." Find comfort in knowing that when your parents or friends get on your case, God is right beside you, loving you, caring for you, looking out for you.

REFLECTION:

1. Is loneliness a normal feeling from time to time?
2. Is loneliness God's idea?

૪ↅ

✔ CHALLENGES:

Try some of our loneliness-busters, the next time you feel down:

- Call a friend and tell her you're lonely.
- Go do something good for someone: help a child fix a broken toy or give your Mom an extra hand with chores.
- Listen to some of your favorite music while you do some exercise—sit ups, jumping jacks, touch-your-toes.

What About Cults?

Perhaps you think you'd never join a cult.

But, unfortunately, that thought doesn't keep some people from joining.

Some cult leaders are clever. They "brainwash" their followers slowly and carefully so the followers can't see what's happening.

Some cult leaders say they are teaching the gospel when, in fact, they are greedy, asking for contributions for their personal needs. Other cult leaders demand sex with one or more cult members. And some cult leaders actually claim to be Jesus Christ.

So why do people join cults?

Different people join for different reasons.

Some say they joined a cult so they could belong to a group. Others say they were distraught and lonely when they joined. Still others say they were attracted to the cult because they were homeless.

Even Satanic cults can be attractive to teens.

One former Satanic-cult member is death-row inmate Sean Sellers, who confessed to killing his parents when he was a teen. He made public statements that he wanted to belong to a group and be powerful.

That's what attracted him to a Satanic cult.

Maybe Sean learned that a cult couldn't give him power or security. He found *that* only in Jesus. But he found it too late to prevent a terrible crime. Today, Sean is on death row at the Oklahoma State Penitentiary.

✝ SCRIPTURE:

"Dear friends, do not believe every spirit, but test the spirits to see whether they are from God, because

many false prophets have gone out into the world."
I John 4:1

REFLECTION:

1) Do you know anyone who is or has been a member of a cult? What drew them to that group?

2) What kind of prevention can you take so you won't become involved in a cult?

✔ CHALLENGE:

Educate yourself on cults by:
- Reading library materials on cults.
- Asking a Christian education person or minister to help you understand more about cults.
- Suggesting a program on cults for your church youth group or Sunday School class.

Strength

I know a Christian teen girl, Janet, who is a runner. She plans someday to enter the Olympics. That's why she gets on the track every day at 6:30 in the morning and runs. When Janet gets tired, she makes herself go an extra lap. "It always amazes me," Janet told me, smiling, "that I seem to have more strength than I realized. That's the way a runner trains. You always go that little extra bit to develop your body. You call on that extra strength. This builds confidence."

"When you enter the Olympics, do you plan on bringing any medals home?" I was curious to know.

Janet smiled. "I don't know. A lot of people enter and only a few can win, but I'm going to try. I'm going to do my best."

Janet is doing exactly what St. Paul told Christians to do in his letter to the Corinthians. See the Bible verse below for details.

Realize that as a Christian you have an inner strength too.

Use it. Go that extra mile in life by calling on Christ for help. When you are tired, either physically or mentally, ask God for extra energy to meet whatever circumstance you have to meet. God wants to help.

† SCRIPTURE:

"Do you not know that in a race all the runners run, but only one gets the prize? Run in such a way as to get the prize. Everyone who competes in the game goes into strict training..." I Corinthians 9:24-25

REFLECTION:

1) Recall a situation where you needed extra strength. Did you call on God for help? Why or why not?

2) Think of a Christian you know who demonstrates an inner strength by her or his daily living. Analyze why that person is succeeding.

✔CHALLENGE:

Compete with others, while remembering only one person can win first place.

For example, if you slaved over your science fair project and didn't place, take pleasure in knowing you entered the contest and did the best you could.

That's all Jesus Christ is asking you to do!

God in Your Life

Keeping God in Your Life

BAD NEWS: Teens live in an age of high crime, national weather disasters and stressful competition at school.

GOOD NEWS: In the midst of this turmoil, you can find strength, courage and peace in Jesus Christ, our Lord!

Remember that.

As a child of God, you are in His safekeeping. It doesn't matter where you are or what is happening. God is always with you. That is a fact. Nothing will ever change that.

Take assurance in this knowledge. Thank God for His protection.

True, we don't know what tomorrow—or the rest of today for that matter—will bring. But with Jesus Christ, the Bible says you can have the strength to face any situation.

What could be more comforting?

✝ SCRIPTURE:

"I will praise the Lord, who counsels me; even at night my heart instructs me. I have set the Lord always before me. Because he is at my right hand, I will not be shaken.

"Therefore my heart is glad and my tongue rejoices; my body also will rest secure, because you will not abandon me to the grave, nor will you let your Holy One see decay. You have made known to me the path of life; you will fill me with joy in your presence, with eternal pleasures at your right hand." Psalm 16:7-11

REFLECTION:

1. Does the world frighten you sometimes? If so, what can you do during these times?

2. Think of ways you can turn to God the next time you're stressed from competition.

✔ CHALLENGE:

Keep God in your life by:

• Praying.

• Reading the Bible.

• Being an active member of a church youth group.

Loving God

How much do you love God?

Probably only you and God know the answer. Christians are to love God more than anything or anyone else.

"Listen, I do that," you may say quickly.

But every now and then it's important for Christians to take an inventory of their Christian lives. Ask yourself questions. Dig into your inner self. Discover how much you love God.

For example: how important is money to you? Can you go without a new pair of shoes or do you feel like you will just die if you can't get them for the party Friday night? Be careful not to let money become a "god" in your life.

Try reading Exodus chapter 32 to see what happened when the Israelites became obsessed with their material possessions.

And remember, these Israelites were not unique. In today's society, people still worship "gods" such as money, popularity, power, or possessions .

So be careful not to let material things—or anything else in your life—become your god.

† SCRIPTURE:

"And God spoke all these words: 'I am the Lord your God, who brought you out of Egypt, out of the land of slavery. You shall have no other gods before me.'" Exodus 20:1-3

REFLECTION:

1) Do you have any "gods" in your life at the present time?

2) If you do, what are they? How can you get rid of them?

❦

🔖 SUGGESTION:

Before you go to bed, pray this prayer:

Please help me in my teen years so I don't worship other "gods" like money or other material things. Help me to appreciate what I have so I don't feel angry if I can't have stuff like designer blue jeans all the time. Let me find the lasting things in life—like your love, grace and assurance. Remind me that that's all I need. Amen.

Faith

Have faith.

Sure, you hear that all the time—from parents, teachers, friends.

It sounds great.

But how can you have faith after you fail that important trig test? Or when your best friend is injured in a car accident? Or when your parents ground you for not coming home on time?

"Exactly how do you have faith then?" you may ask.

True, it's not easy to have faith when everything in your world turns upside down. But it can be done.

"Listen, that sounds great, but my faith hasn't amounted to a whole lot lately," you may admit.

That's okay.

Remember, you don't need much faith to develop positive attitudes in your mind. In Matthew 17:20 Jesus says, "Because you have so little faith. I tell you the truth, if you have faith as small as a mustard seed, you can say to this mountain, 'Move from here to there' and it will move. Nothing will be impossible for you."

Sometime take a look at a mustard seed. It's not big.

Also, sometime read the faith chapter, Hebrews 11, to learn about the faith some people had in Biblical times.

† SCRIPTURE:
"Now faith is being sure of what we hope for and certain of what we do not see. " Hebrews 11:1

REFLECTION:

1) Recall a situation where you had faith to cope through the struggle. How did God help?

2) Think of a Christian you know who has a lot of faith. How would you describe that person? Easy going? Pleasant to be around? Looks on the bright side?

✤

✔ CHALLENGE:

In Romans 10:17 it says, "Consequently, faith comes from hearing the message, and the message is heard through the word of Christ."

• Make it a daily habit to remind yourself that faith comes from God and cannot be physically seen. Ask for God to give you faith.

• Put a faith-builder in your life today by stopping right now at this very moment to be still.

• Close your eyes and listen for Christ's message, remembering that we do not have to hear an audible voice from God, that He communicates by thought.

Prayer

Every Christian needs a good prayer life.

How is your prayer life?

To answer that question, analyze the way you talk to God.

After all, that's exactly what prayer is—talking to God.

Are you in a hurry when you pray, anxious to get to a friend's house or go out for pizza? Do you even pray when you are feeling good and everything is okay in your world? Or are your prayers full of panic, last minute bits of dialog with God when you're ready to take a test or give a speech?

Make sure you include God in all the aspects of your life.

He cares. He wants to hear from you.

Don't be concerned about what you say or how to say it when you pray. God isn't fussy about grammar. You don't have to speak with "thous" like the Biblical people did. Speak in your normal everyday language to God.

Include God in everything you do. Ask for His direction.

Give thanks for the blessings in your life. Don't hesitate to call on Him when you're having a bad day.

Do this and you will have a good prayer life.

✝ SCRIPTURE:

"If my people, who are called by my name, will humble themselves and pray and seek my face and turn from their wicked ways, then will I hear from heaven and will forgive their sin and will heal their land." II Chronicles 7:14

REFLECTION:

1) Why is prayer important?

2) How would you rate your prayer life? Good? Or a little on the weak side? How can you make it stronger?

✔ SUGGESTION:

Pray—talk—to God sometime today. Tell Him how you are feeling and how your day is going. God cares.

Having trouble getting started? Simply complete this prayer, filling in the blanks with your personal concerns:

Hi God,

The best thing that happened to me today was

_____.

And the worst thing was _____.

Please give me the guidance I need.

The biggest problem in my life right now is

_____.

Please help me with that problem, Lord. In Jesus name.

Amen.

Are You Listening, Lord?

About the Author

In *Are You Listening, Lord?*, free-lance writer Mary Ann Kerl engages her young readers in meaningful reflections and challenges.

Mrs. Kerl is a newspaper correspondent for *Tusla World*. She has an impressive array of more than 1,000 magazine and newspaper articles that have been published in such widely-read magazines as *Family Circle, Home Life, Virtue, High Adventure, Living With Children, Lady's Circle, Venture, Touch, Jack and Jill, The Writer,* and many other national as well as international publications.

Are You Listening, Lord? is Mary Ann's fifth book. Her new three-book series titled *The OK! Kids* is set in Oklahoma and will be released soon. She has written children's Sunday School curriculum materials for United Methodist Publishing House that will be used to the turn of the century.

A creative writing instructor, Mrs. Kerl earned her degrees in journalism and home economics from South Dakota State University in Brookings. She is an ordained deacon in the Presbyterian church. She makes her home in McAlester, Oklahoma, with Bob, her husband of 27 years. They have two grown sons.